Her Various Scalpels

Also by Sophie Mayer:

(as Sophie Levy)
Marsh Fear/Fen Tiger (2002, with Leo Mellor)
These Are the Licks (2003)
junkmaildays (2004)

Forthcoming
The Cinema of Sally Potter: A Politics of Love (2009)
The Private Parts of Girls (2010)

There She Goes: Feminist Filmmaking and Beyond
    (Ed., with Corinn Columpar) (2009)

SOPHIE MAYER

Her Various Scalpels

Shearsman Books
Exeter

First published in the United Kingdom in 2009 by
Shearsman Books Ltd
58 Velwell Road
Exeter EX4 4LD

www.shearsman.com

ISBN 978-1-84861-040-8

Copyright © Sophie Mayer, 2009.
First Edition

The right of Sophie Mayer to be identified as the author of this work has been asserted by her in accordance with the Copyrights, Designs and Patents Act of 1988. All rights reserved.

Acknowledgements:
Several of these poems appeared previously, some in different versions, some with different titles. My thanks (alphabetically) to the editors of the following journals, for publication opportunities and editorial advice: *Blackbox Manifold, Brand, Chroma, Iota, Masthead, nth position, Shearsman, Stand, Staple, Stride, Twelfth Street Review, West Coast Line, zafusy.*

'No Such Thing' collates excerpts from *Filmgrimage*, a series of photo-essays with images by Lady Vervaine, published in *Vertigo*, issues 3.1 (Summer 2006) through 3.7 (Autumn 2007). 'Je Suis Ici' was written in response to a scenario and rough cut of *Je Suis Ici*, a short film by Ben Crowe and Preti Taneja. 'You Are Here' formed part of *Wänderland*, a promenade show performed by Wingspan (Doug McCabe, Sophie Mayer, Debs Paterson, Davina Silver and Zoë Svendsen) in Cambridge, July 2000.

Cover image:
Elena Ray: 'Abstract Tree Collage'.
Copyright © Elena Ray, 2005.

Contents

Her Various Scalpels   9

the star poems
    Self Portrait as Supernova   13
    Carbon Dating   15
    Rearranging the Stars   20
    Star Power   21
    Stuff for Making the Shapes of Stars   23
    Lampyridae   24
    Shell Like   26

Miss Tinguette   28
The Day Antonioni Died   29
Import/Export   31
No Such Thing   34

Two Scenarios for Short Films
    Je Suis Ici   39
    You Are Here   41

Lèche Vitrine   47
Sleepside   56
Blackouts   58
Unwing   62
The Burning Girls: A Novel   64

the cock poems
    instrument / mouth   71
    Imagine / arm   73
    bliss / skin   74
    Bourgeois / foreskin   75
    promises / eye   76

Nobody Knows / ankles   78
London Fashion Week / pelvis   80
zero degrees / navel   81
pieuvres / lèvres (lilies / lips)   82

For all the stargazers – friends and strangers – who've shared the dark.

Her Various Scalpels

I tell you: I was born
like a knife—all folded—

the rest—I learned. What
you call surface is

space—slotted—with blades.
Its sense of—retractable—its edge

imperceptible. We live by—prepositions
& are mineral—the talent of smoke

in an era of shine. And if I
run a current—

and if I run
a gauntlet—and if red appears

upon it—that is

the flick—and
silver—

over. My trick
blade.

the star poems

Self-Portrait as Supernova
after Lynne Stopkewich's Kissed

I have been so many things: girl, book, bird-
bone, soft fur. All blood

and cotton packing: life marks death at fingertip.
What little we know a trap

admitting no light. Or spring: a tulip,
slender as rain, unshrugs burlap.

Petals against my thigh. He died, yes, and
what was cold in him called

through me, always opening without end
in luminescence. What cannot be held

happens whitely from skin and eye: heat
death, dense at the core, iron heart

imploding. Wave after white wave repeat-
ing evacuation. I am down to parts:

palms, lips, voice. A nerve cluster trembling,
pulsing at the edge of seen. Bang

they name this: this imperceptible furling
of light against light. Blaze what longs,

like comets trailing night's black minute,
scars of gas and flame, so determined

and so free. And in the after,
nothing much. My little art—

release, light as laughter.
Echoes all that last.

Carbon Dating
after Michael Winterbottom's 9 Songs

1.
Nothing much remains.
Carbon, trace of her

burn in me, is all. Exhale once,
twice, again, and it is gone

almost, hanging before my
furred mouth, a cloud

in which I see our residue,
entwining.

2.
That thing a star does with itself
is night. Is irising against

the night in swirls of blaze,
mirror of the watching eye

below it, cast into frigid awe
and molten want, as gaze

coils between open and
open.

3.
Rock. Star. Elements
in any form, coming

together. Small talk like
radiation, reaction, the fight

against gravity. Her fingers
are glowsticks, their length

tastes of sweat, smoke, iron:
heavy metals.

4.
And in her, a universe and
an age. Why range only in

space? Whorled. Mine, she is,
and striated, so I trace her

history, bury myself in her—
take the tarnish off these

phrases in our translucent
newness.

5.
Unknown quantities. In close
proximity: circle, attract, approach,

implode. Reform. A haze about
her—something undiscovered,

off the chart. Under the table.
Against the wall. Everywhere

we can enter each other, gaseous,
nebulous.

6.
And in our orbit, our stately,
violent passing, our horizon-

tal pas-de-deux, the music
of the spheres. Aurora

australis, the rending
of the sky: cold lightning

in widescreen, some shaking.
Handheld.

7.
History is littered with fools
following their stars. Dis-

asters. Burnings and explosions,
distress flares that lead searchers

to skeletons. And in the bones
a spark that speaks, in tongues—

concentric, lapping, porous—of the
heart.

8.
What chokes us, too, is
carbon. Hides the night sky,

blurs outlines. Cigarettes and
cars. Our fault, then. Here, where

all is white, I've come to see
clearly: her million points of light,

scintillating silver knives, rushing
past.

9.
Or from the past. Look up,
see memory: the universe

swishing slow in its developing
tray, brilliant chemical bath

for sore eyes. Click. What was
between us, between us forever.

Frozen moments moving, warmed
by breath.

Rearranging the Stars
after Anthony Minghella's The English Patient

Lost you. Out here, where a call to prayer shivers
stone into song, where night falls like knives,

there's a trick to the sky, how you see it, smell
what's coming. It is like reading. It's so small

at first, and granular, then overwhelms: eyes,
mouth, hands, hair. You cannot possibly sleep.

But you do, lulled by wind and waking. Stories—
his stories, more stories than there could be stars—

breathe around you with their shine, draw hearts
on dirty glass. You know what they find in deserts:

fragments. Texts under sand winds, brilliant disasters.
And you, in secret, on fire with new constellations.

Star Power
after Sally Potter's The Gold Diggers

Night finds out the gold in us,
a skin thing: you laugh and

your laugh is liquid
assets. What gilds

corrodes. You're the red
in the landscape: the seam,

the stream. Rust tests
your mettle, copper

to the tongue. What
does a star wish on?

How does a star
turn itself on?

It's been said you're made
of stone. Of glass. Of ice.

You've been rendered
speechless. It's a stitch-up.

All this brilliance
a sequined costume

for the headline:
we are here. And we

burn. Unshaken,
we are ghosts of it,

fragments and pale
imitators, as stars are:

gas and grit and mystery
and velocity. Our speed

is light.

Stuff for Making the Shape of Stars
after Rebecca Miller's The Ballad of Jack and Rose

And then, where to keep them: here,
beside this box of snakes, a barrel of light.

The wood that built my bird-house
heart. I cannot part myself

from you—always see you imprinted
through the sky. My constellation.

My fragments, half-formed, home
movies. Old hat. And that it's yours

what counts, your press of bone, thin
as tinder under fires I want to set.

Not once, the night sky (eclipsed
by stupid tripping, all that bright

of headlights). Not once the kiss.
And so I tear up and keep it

torn: the sound of your voice, spilt
coffee, gasoline. The garden I planted.

The lungs you have emptied.
Our silence. Our last chance

for flight. Smoke disappearing.
See: I'm projecting

an old film, flickering
fire.

LAMPYRIDAE
    after Sofia Coppola's The Virgin Suicides

Fireflies are the only insects that can flash their light in distinct signals

watch for lightning, astral
configurations,
flickering of lava lamps

against lace curtains. these
our signals.
binoculars, seismometers,

guitars: we are male and
instrumental
and do not understand them,

even over the microscope in
chem lab.
they resist all experiments.

    The females remain in the larval state and are called glowworms

as boys, we kept them
in jars,
summers before the trees

began to die. paradise
lost. grade
twelve, mrs. deakin's english

class. it strikes a chord
we played
out endlessly, imitating Dylan,

Hendrix, Wilson, anyone
not our
fathers, who we have become.

Light production in these creatures is still not completely understood

we will never stop missing
them, always
arrive too late and not save

ourselves. bioluminescence
will break
against us each summer,

ghosts of white dresses
at dusk.
our sisters, wives, daughters, lovers

each carry within them our
broken hearts:
inexplicable, larval, glowing. theirs.

see them make holes in the dark

Shell Like

after Lucrecia Martel's La Niña Santa

The sky holds mother's milk. Sweet

isn't it, like the knees of a girl who
has knelt only to Jesus. And what

she's told him while she's there, pouring
herself into his perfect ear. That holy

orifice, punctuated by an asterisk
of dark where confession disappears,

where whispers sound an echo
to the stars. Is he hollow—you know,

like an Easter egg—the man case
moulded around the impossible

plastic of the divine. Do we rattle
in him: all our lies, our prayers,

our little waves of need. Hush.
The shore of solace. Water

listens: lapping, rushing. Soft
bodies aloft on breath, on

chlorine, turn like planets.

Miss Tinguette

'A kiss can be a comma, a question mark, or an exclamation mark.'

These are my legs, these my lips:
grace is punctuation. I was Paris, said
Maurice (and who can you trust if not
a Chevalier?). I took his name
for me, lightly, a Parisian *baise*. Yes, I know
its double meaning, wear
rouge and feathers and fantails
and not much else. Eyebrows like commas.

' "Innocent Eyes" on my tongue became "Innocent Asses." '

Au clair de la lune: New York aglow
with my leaving. From the boat, it is
a giant cabaret, buildings shimmying
and waltzing. Oh, for stockings fine
as night air. For silence, between my eye
and the camera. For the slippery moment of *yes,
oui, oeil, eyes, asses*. Assets. Nothing
innocent plays about my lips.

'I say "Come closer" and draw them to me.'

For my legs, 500, 000 francs. For my lovers,
kings and princes, singers and audiences and
no-one. Jeanne Bourgeois. I told no-one. Silent
in film after film, all that remains of me now
is nothing. A few photographs, vinyl whisperings,
a feather. Unmissed if unmistakable. Spoken for,
so to speak, by a chorus of those I thought
I'd left behind. Those who hold my train.

The Day Antonioni Died

> The future that was the intensely heartfelt focus
> of Mozart's aspirations during his last days on
> earth has become our present.
> —Peter Sellars

Breakfast of salmon and Bergman obituaries. And after,
checking email to the sound of a new CD—
Jocelyn Pook, angelic as if angels were messengers of (not air
but) fire, volcanic—over which, your cry, eclipsing.

Another one gone. I walk out into the sun (what a gift after
weeks of rain, unseasonal, snails on the doorstep each damp
evening), phone Maxie about *Carmen* while the W5 doesn't come,
thinking about Act III: Carmen sees her own death. On stage,

death will dance in black and spangles, threading tango back
into its intricate origins. Her name means *song*, means *magic*
and that's how tonight (Rokia Traore, *Wati*, Barbican 7.30 pm,
booked online) we'll celebrate not her last acts, but Mozart's. Late

style like this late summer with its dozy bees gathering their
own death. Call it *Eros* or New Crowned Hope. Call it Mozart
as griot to the court of Sundiata. Or the ache
in Billie's late recordings. It's too warm for this blazer, autumn

grey shading into the silver-black of my dress. I'm the moon
to your red-golden Sun Ra T-shirt, but when night falls I'll shiver
deliciously in the enveloping cool, passing from light into darkness
as we leave the Turkish store with a new kind of hummus

that is that rarest of things: as good as it sounds on the label.
Cuminative, we joke, its taste as precise as the shadows limned by

the street's moon illusion. Golden, just off the true: soft
as the blood orange jelly we ate for dessert, in the uncomfortable

company of your cousin. *There's hardly any white people downtown,
do you know what I mean?* Oh, but we understand something
    different
by it: us. Rush of tongues through markets, radios alive with drums
from another world. Which is also this one. Always. We meet

in the centre, settle in plush seats at 7.27. London—east—I walked
it crabwise, past Shoreditch Halal Grocery on streets where
my great-grandparents sold *schmattes*. Passengers poured from taxis
into a molten afternoon. Sun drops west to where you walked

before our love. Streets of *Blow Up*'s swing, now hung with clothes
that cost a bomb. But the city gathers us where Malian desert
flares the screen behind Rokia Traoré's voice, which has room for
    us all, room even for the ghost
of Billie Holiday, who died alone at 44. And if she were a griotte

six hundred years ago, grown old praising kings? Men grow old
and die. Maybe Godard will be next, or Miyazaki. Don't worry:
there'll be a season. Maybe even for Sembène, griot rioting
in the colonial heart. Maybe Billie will walk before his ghost,
    praising the night.

Import/Export

Late/x

Apparent is (apparently) enough. An extra *p* I feel beneath the mattress, all talk of readiness to take the plunge. But here in rubber sheeting, we have no ointment for that rash. How careless to become so irritated. Such a sap to crack at such viscosity. Imported what's important. Substitutes are military. Are susceptible. Are not available free at this surgery. Our wrecking ball comes first, all edginess and walls of flame. When lip slips. His squeak between. The gap that nothing whistled through. Will not regenerate. Pink water and the glitter inside whose descent unleashes. Punchline missed in the trawl for bone. Cracked and glazed. Illegal fish from coastal waters. It's getting late. Clock that: the rising seas will take their bow. Iridescent, the broken vow of care. Disrupted sleep. The flood of dreams. Potential clouds. Reform. And pour again, this time to pool. To crystallise in duct formations, neuronal synthesis. Of this: the sheet grows taut, a drumstruck skin. Resonance is distant, backward echo rising through the muffle. From whose perspective. The pea speaks. Her sleeping restless weight. And in the damp of morning, all is red disguised as white. Those patches there, they'll scar. Be seen, unsheathed and from the sky.

Theobroma

Foundation: bean from seed. Dark husk discarded for the meat. And sweetness, added all too soon, a cane for jaded palates. Continents as packaged goods: wrapped in gold and ribbon-tied, to give the lie when rot sets in. Abundance. None forged cleanly, powder and crumb littering the floor. And now they trade fair claims: scatter the sacred and consumed. How flattering. Presented as collection. No trifle. As always, dark liquid turned to gold and so to art. Masonry of slab and bar. The halls to house the world with what's been taken. A moulded, fluted cake: surprise inside. And he who breaks his tooth, and she who chokes it down, shall be crowned the king and queen. Shall wear silver and purple crowns. Shall be foiled, stained with what melts. Blooms to white at their heated touch.

Cha

It is a ceremony of conjoinment and as one: black into white. Or otherwise. The swirl. The vows of steam. Fluctuant inhalation. Centrifuge with careful water and embrace. Burn to touch (through glass, clay, polymer or foam) and move away. Takeout. Must leak in order to become, must intervene but not dissolve. Dispersal as principle, molecular intermingling run up against borders (glass, clay, polymer or foam). So each different curvature will meet your hand, and each finger has its own behaviour. Though not cosmetic. Though it will dye. Stains the dry maps of once, preceding. Is all talk. Some say with salt and some with lemon. Some with rancid butter and some with wads of paper. Such healing for such great harm. Bricked as money. Picked under the sun and endlessly. Whiff of city port lands, ghost stream. Marsh flavour. Each cup contains its future, wet and fuming. To say nothing of its lumps. Such quiet silver to be so uncontained, a matted history (twist, uncover) remains when you are done.

No Such Thing

"Les travellings sont affaires de morale."
Jean-Luc Godard, 1960

Filmgrimage

[Earliest use in English, 1205. From Old Fr. *pelegrin*. From Latin *peregrinum*, one who comes from foreign parts. *Per* (through) + *ager* (fields, lands). Wanderer, religious traveller, colonist, falcon]

wander through the [visual] field
travel with film in mind

Montréal

Pèlerimage. Film is a foreign land we come through.
A foreign land where we come to.

We confuse the places we dreamed with the places we walk.
They lie over one another, a slender archaeology.

If I stand on the right corner and look, I will step in through the lens of the camera.
Aperture.
Yes. An opening. Opening something in me.
Open. But empty.
The film? It's all around us.
The place. The church. Like a tomb.
So much to see ...
Nothing. At the tomb of the film the body was gone.

Glasgow

> The city/screen takes on
> a double meaning:
>
> Entrance.
> Refuse.
>
> The screen a
> window barred.
>
> There is no outside
> only frames within frames.

Paris

You write to me from the end of cinema. I see it: the leader winding through the projector, clicking like a stone against pavement. Love is a fear that takes hold of the city: the screen will tear. Can you see the space that will show? Such questions, like kisses, leave me breathless.

Iceland

It is so cold that speech is impossible. The landscape breathes words of ice and fire. With picks and maps, we go looking. See signs. *Here Be Monsters*. Geysirs. Glaciers. Volcanoes.

Rainbows. Cinema speaks in signs: each can be mined for meaning. The landscape is impossible. With fire and ice, it writes and erases the story. Here be angles, edges, frames.

Teeth chattering, we approach. See films
in the Northern Lights. Myth, riddle, rune. Score
images on bone. Mouth strange songs sung to drums.

Let them escape on our breath when we wake.

Dungeness

His teaching: as simple as stone. Here
he said. Cool against skin. A dream

of colours. Cast it in anger, or plant it
in the mud. Do neither. Hold,

hold until you know its shape.
Then carve it. Set it alight.

Two Scenarios for Short Films

JE SUIS ICI

Intro: driving through vineyards. Music: Edith Piaf. Jaunty.
Where are we? *Ici.* Here. At last. After
here in my phrase book: hot. House.
                Then hungry.

1. *A mountain village—*
I am learning the words of things: *montagne,*
magasin. Fermé. Still a shop when it's closed?
The street is empty with. *Pierres. Chiens. Soleil.*
Comprenez-vous français? I wish I knew the French
                for swallow.

2. *A market.*
Marché. Also, *marcher:* to walk. *Ça marche bien.*
It goes well. I walk. My stride rhythmic:
Bien. Rien. Can you eat a smell? A taste?
                A place?

3. *A pristine untouched salad.*
Plat: a plate or meal. But more.
Art, the placement *comme ça.* Angles. Muscles. Flesh.
Fresh. Untouched. If I eat, will this be *ici*
                forever?

4. *Van Gogh Café, Arles.*
Days proceed by frames: windows (car, hotel, café).
By guidebook, painting, memory, viewfinder, postcard.
Frame. *Fermé.* Everything here seen a million times.
        Take it.

5. *Looking through cards with a pot of salt to hand.*
Sel. Once currency. Pot of gold to stop
meat from turning. Like love: keeps things fresh,
red and present. Fire. Running through me—
freshwater worth its salt. A day's grain (or
grace). Its taste. The touch of it to
        my tongue.

6. *Salt mountains seen from a fortress whose shadow on ramparts looks like teeth.*
Bite into blue. Make dents. Impossible. Untouchable.
All I have wanted: sky, sun. To see
the frame. And beyond it. To open
the eyes of my brightest wings and turn
        my face

7. *She licks the stamp and places it on the blank card before posting.*
        (in)to the sun.

You Are Here

The City Once

Every city is terrifying.

Because of this, avenues of trees are rushed by twilight,

and bells are the sound of roses opening too early,
but surviving the frost.

Because of this, anecdotal evidence for love
is carried by pigeon from wall to wall

and is written in the Surrealist manifesto of raindrops
on windows,

and because of this, trees, bells, flowers, windows, birds, frost
       and rain

all open their hearts like ears, dilating,
to catch the sound of a wingbeat.

Or is it sunset.

There is no concrete evidence
for the ground you stand on.

Every city is an iceberg,
scintilla of snow angels,

every story we tell.

Aevum

[n. (of time) a wingspan]

Angels with ice-cream tongues
press 'play' on the taped bird calls

and we come flocking. Stars fall
between trees and become glass:

windows, champagne, a shivering.
A feather, flame. Dangerous walks

through kitchen graveyards, through the sound of a garden
sea. Through portals, through camera lenses.

The upside-down sensation of passing through an angel,
their eye a torn-out space of blue.

Epithalamium

Marry words to vision: this conceptual wedding
of the allegorical   *to the real*

or, say, welding
the bright arc of gold, the not putting asunder
smile embracing smile

hands clasped to catch whatever falls.
Tears. Confetti.
The sun

touching its glowing tip to the inertia of land.

What catches fire.
The spaces of light in her hair,

the first recorded marriage song.
Principle of saffron and pitch-flame.

The earth hugs into night.

Under their wedding dresses, the girls go barefoot,
soaking the last heat of stone through their skin.

Nothing but rain now, black falling
with silver. Under their dresses,

the girls wear invisible wings.

Mir/or/and/a

      —turning away from her father's books (no
      pictures or conversations) she falls—

her eyelid a butterfly
just opening the chrysalis of her eye

her eye a bird tumbled from the nest of her face. first flight.

you girl in the glowing dress,
turn yourself down.
neither the time not the place.

her mouth mouthing her lines,
swallowing them—

gill, gull, gullet, gullible, cuttable, gutted

fish for breakfast, fish for lunch, fish for dinner
her earliest memory. *our children would be half-sea
selkies* she thinks, catching her fingers on the upward
cut of his scales.

but the white rabbit
spirits her away

o! wonderland, to have such mirrors in it

Swan Shift

These words cannot touch you
until you reach your hands   out
(light behind)
and I see the bones in them
are wings'
tips
last leap of the old once-were game
in shoulder blades
remaining
what we once were and could do
awake in us still

vestigial,

Lèche Vitrine (A Ballet)

> I am letting you into the secret of all secrets:
> mirrors are gates through which death comes and goes.
> —Jean Cocteau, *Orphée*

i. allusive

                    carry glass on my back

the mercury slippage
alchemical dawn whose lustral   cinema

                              seditious
her evening   gloved as   sheets of an earlier

he will look back   *pages of earlier*   are   *moth wings*
        leave dusty prints of   touch
                              and die

ii. bifurcate

              defensive Rorschachs
    walk in pairs from the earliest
    such is couplet   in the night mirror

    we meet   stunned
    into flutter
                across spinal likeness
        devolve

            each nautilus of brain   each coil
                  we have time
                second   hands

iii. epiphanic

        a torque of
                she speaks of hold and we
              in your shell like echoes ridged

                    we fold and fold these
                        body parts
                  reflexive/studio-mirror

            axis the muscles step into one-two
                    footprints on the floor

iv. hendiadys

        tongues butterfly

   in such words

as   *the whole tongue of you parts my wings*

as   *eyes*
              winged   *[no defences]*
                  closed

as   *the body rhythmic*   *night moth against glass*

as   *febrile joining*

as
                    shut up and kiss me

v. instigate
> *these mirrors for which we are unprepared*

fold back density of sand
experimental glass

        desert windowed by airborne gaze

vi. mnemonic
                      glass muscled
flex   unlikely torsion   coils of   glow and souvenir

        we receive our finest thoughts through radio

binocular perspective on the blank book   such brilliance
                                                          reflective glare
        which stores these frames
        cells brushed from your body

        salt and transparent as wings

vii. pellucid
brushing dust across supercooled

     these need to be echoed
          curvilinear   aural forms : lobe
                                                  auricle
                                              tympanum
cochlear your   favourite   we repeat
                               operate   in pairs

        surrealist angels of history   or not
                                                  voluptuary
night as coil, receiving
through glass in   cars of black and white

viii. suspension
                disclose across nerves

          is in tears
    falling

in each drop her   tiny   reflection
                                    holds   to downy skin
[my childhood memory
                opens in your mouth]
                                    in the studio mirror

      porte de bras   holding   my own
                              [hand   spasms
                                en pointe

                                                    and flex—
ix. windlass
                        that no two mouths

would you look back   at prints pressed into   glass my look-back
                            alchemy

receptors taste each   lepidopterists of kiss

five positions of the spine
                in most avian species, it is the male who performs

                    the folds of your flesh disclose
                    radio silence I carry away on fingertips
                    echoed long mirrors in the darkness of a room

Sleepside

Cloned from a crumb of sleep
    I speak as dream-self
                for the union of dream selves;
you have made us
    metal and flesh, erratic sculptures
                tilting in another wind.
Come in.

This is our last resort
    and yours—tissue of lost
                hope. The sheets. Shed skin
of which we are composed
    and recomposed—such waste
                recycled into haunted things.
Come in

and make yourselves
    unhomely. That room you will
                remember, whose furniture
rearranged (mahogany to
    melancholy) is shadow
                pocketed. Where you begin,
come in,

for if we don't invite you,
    you will invade. Colonise
                our shadows as your shadow
selves. We are your night, and its
    associations. Dirty insomnias,
                your emptiness projecting:
come in.

And so we fill the crevices
        you evacuate. We are subdermal,
                      febrile, viral
with our eloquence. Articulations
        itching, you scratch red to
                      find us, grinning—
Come in.

BLACKOUTS

1.
labour day, bleak and strewn
one more rolling   apocalypse

the summer it all ended
every week   a new episode

our reality show eliminating   breathing
swimming, eating

light   the city
stunned into plague carnival

proverbial flesh and rush of Pride
wedding earth and sky   with a rainbow

band, Caribana rain sizzling on barbecues
dancers' bodies slicked   for the Sun Queen

we take our pleasures as   forecast
I ♥ TORONTO totes toting sunscreen and umbrellas

tokens of our appropriation   by provincial declaration
we must be tourists in our own backyard

scarred by corporate branding
neon signs returning   to light

amassing like storm clouds overhead
we ready ourselves for   the fall

one last call   at the
long weekend bar, airshow at the Ex, planes

rip the sky the subway   underfoot echo
on not being able to sleep my bedside reading

in this wet remnant of swelter, blistered with sweat
ice cream tubs in a blackout   pocking in the half-dark

romanced by candles, we smell of burning
wax on skin, news of   forest fires

shares its singe we   sleep fitfully
without a/c and dream, despite ourselves

& careful tans,   in ice
and winter *oh I wish I had a river I could skate away on*

2.
should know better than this obsessive checking of email
with my edges

still wet from sleeping off
that

shorting out the cool air and opening the silent sky
to star punctures

pointillist shadings of a tattoo
gun I felt in my bones

you were coming
for me

morning flashes up your proof of words
splashed like sweat

on the screen my skin constellations of goosebumps
paled by neon

alerts blurring my vision with contradictions
delete undelete expunge

you revive in me the sheer wall of *coruscating* its sound
adolescent and rebarbative

everything is noir and loud as *Blade Runner*
everything is advertising

what I should buy into
your letter your

love your definition thereof as nine-tenths
of the law

whose words, reversed, mark on me in blue who this song
was never for

3.

All the names are the fathers', and none of them are real. The letters are all false despite the stamp, zygotic. Not known at this address. Reaching out to mailer-daemons. Encryption or kryptonite. As cheesecloth is to ectoplasm. These things do come up. (A stain, some seepage). Swallow my tongue—curative—a grated root. No ifs or cuts. Left to loss of face I'd take the sword before the knife. Hand over mouth. No more than a number-plate, a round of mumbledypeg. And they stumble over me still: all careless vowels left echoing. No words fingerprinted in the breath on the mirror. You are smoke at sunset. Like the book says. For on the seventh day. For our sins. Forenames taken from and inscribed therein. Distillation of years, a rendering. Offered up. Grease and ash and fat, and lumps of final bone.

Unwing

In certain dreams, I have a house made of paper and barbed wire. The paper is watermarked bond. The house (as I understand it) is inside me and light glows through the rip. To be a house made of wings is the idea but I cannot get the cage to fit. There are precedents. Ties to history. Look. She places the straps over her dress and washes her doll in the morning light. She will call him: a single note, missing. Winging the question of water, what we see without. And through. Just a droplet, forming.

Between her shoulder blades. Could a bird rest there, claws delicate as twisting barbs, before pulsing through the vertical. Dust of the uprush. Tear in your hand. You say you'd like ash from my eyelash but it's my flight. It's here in the room. It's soft furnishing and it needs to be vacuumed. Grey pillows will neither hollow nor silver, whatever the moonlight. You cannot mine them, you cannot leave deposits in their seams and return to prise them from my gullet. I have risen, you see, neither bird nor man. On this attenuated plane, I am hovering. I am on wing. I am Mercury.

But reverie spills like saliva from the corner of my mouth. Cigarette sticks. Dribble of ash. For once and all, this is not my skin you're burning; scraped of barnacles, it is within me. Counter-element. Riptide. Full moon for the bird-girl, selkie, phoenix, city. Your wire vibrates with me: furled there amidst your dank pelt, it nestles. Whispers, a thin filament hearing my refusal. So you don't have to. So nothing goes through. You. Become an alley where a bird alighted. Took flight and its echoes. I cannot leave you shit-stained. Not even.

Not obscured. Not, as yet, filed for future reference. I furrow the public archive, exhume its index. It does not point at you. The bars are bars, not arrows. Not lines. Hell, angels I can repel like lightning but the limitless blank of the page sends grey pouring through my ears. All lash and struggle, I lick my lead pencil. For tradition, and the poison. And watermarked. I unwing.

The Burning Girls: A Novel

Medea

Here is how it begins:
        In the morning, the stink of the
        man-boat awakes her.

★

walking lightly, silk-shod, she slips—the youngest—
into her father's study and takes down his dictionary. leaves flutter,

paper crisps to carbon as she reads

awake (v.): (refl.) to arise; (trans.) to arouse

the sultry tongue of it is in her, around her—
torqued, a bangle—at birth—annealed to her wrist.
★
INT. Palace. Day.

Wherever he looks, he sees
gold. And he looks   at her
exotic flashing darkness, livid.
Already she has left him far behind.

Light rides in her sparking hair,
a chariot of the sun.
★
INT. Palace. Night.

He looks up. He looks down.

Her feet are so bare they stun him from her nakedness.
Wreathed in black like a line drawing, she awakes

him to the confluence
of their desires.

His hand is in the crease between her
buttock and thigh.
The pines of Pelion ship their oars,

sigh smooth wood against smooth wood.
The scent of olive oil rises between them,

blue smoke from a skillet. Burnt offering.
★

    She heard the rain before she felt it on her skin; felt
it in her bones before the clap-glamour of clouds had even
rustled up an answer to her spell.
    Yes.
    They would sail out under a storm.
★

    He hears her footsteps in the fall of the rain, and,
against his better judgement, ships his oars. Against his wishes,
he would almost say. Were he as articulate as she, whose
tongue is the strongest muscle in her body.
    He grips the oar handles to stop himself shuddering.
She steps into the dark of the hold. Of his hold. Too dark to
notice that the slick on her is not the sex-wet of summer rain.
The blood heat anneals their bodies like poison.
    What memories, the voyage out, the honeymoon
cruise, her body marked with the grain of him from days of
rowing, rowing. She paints her eyes with kohl and the other
sailors know her for—
    Silence is an outline of her, pen-and-ink of a bird in
flight drawing the whole ocean up after her.
    Her little weather is death.
★

Circe

And C—shesheshe—

> *the one who left before*
> *eldest and*
> *the one who*

she writes them:
> ALL MEN ARE PIGS
>> tattoos her biceps with sailors
>> drinks rum taken from shipwrecks
>> speaks in signs and wonders
>
> THIS ISLAND'S MINE

she is the whirlpool

*

> *she has more*
> *magic in her*
> *little finger*

she defines alone
> NO MAN IS MY ISLAND
>> eats with her fingers
>> dances with a noise like bones
>> sings sea shanties
>
> BLOW THE MAN DOWN

she is as good as her word

*

> *the one who cast*
> *her spell like nets*
> *and pulled*

she mouths a lithe verb
> WANT TAKE HAVE
>> knots her own nets
>> arches against her bonds

                                                                                 blesses the ties
                    OPEN ALL HOURS
she flashes neon fire
★
                                                                                 shine
                                                                              —on—

the cock poems

INSTRUMENT / MOUTH

Anyways. Her most
used phrase, the way she

plays her body a cello
of bone and horse

and string, a trembling
hand she crumples

the new with into the
known when she asks for

music and they bring
her water, she asks

for louder, clouds in
amniotic waves

of vertical that turn screen
to shore, crash tides

under a caustic moon
for the rebel arouser

Death is a sailor
a skinny eclipse

her clarinet
is an axe

it's a hatchet, a cock, a
great tall building

whose falling timbre
is dawn, a cell dividing

and her travels
are her way home

Imagine / arm

Open calls to open, geographically: draw a longitude and
there—across the waves—in a snowstorm of light—she sings
to the glitterball. What she brings from its streets. Phallic
attitude. A body a guitar. A voice and a pulsing left arm.
The sign of a fist, thrust of a strum. Each finger of the left a
blowtorch to the strings.

Strung between land and sky, the tower is all: pointing finger,
Viđey's mooring point for aliens and Vikings, lost foot of
that compass across the water mapping peace. Icicle alive to
gravity's irony. A glass nail defying the hammer. Reaching, it
undoes the pale horizon as fireworks do: electric, unstable, a
scribble of flux.

The lift of the torch begins in her pillowed lip as the curve of
the flames reflect the flow of her Liberty bodice. What thrusts
into the sky is soft as bronze, melting clouds with its heat.
Orgasmic, she is (misread as) erection. Is everything after. She
is surge, holding, streaming, point of return, the musculature
of open.

BLISS / SKIN

> For [Michelangelo], in the last coil of his longing,
> Creation meant everything imaginable being born,
> thrusting and flying, from between men's legs!
> —John Berger

Longing coils
like skin—peeling thin in scratched strips
curled as celluloid.

And fronded: human as vegetal, alive
at its greenest
in a green shade. A border runs through this Eden

but skin does
not stop. Skin is not a line crossed, a wrong fruit
eaten. Everything

imaginable is made from skin. Light is
thrusting and flying
against green, loud as machines, coursing like the river he is

borne on.
Born between thighs, her thumb is the whirl
of that nothing

before the garden. Lifting, he is a river giving
birth or bursting
like a tomato shrugs its skin: shocked into being

fruit. Eaten
in the garden. Until she is all
him.

Bourgeois / foreskin

The penis is capacious: it's a handbag, an armpit,
the space between two objects. Two lips.

Room inside for a lipstick, wallet, tampons,
a gun. Cocked. Dirty tissues, a dried-up pen, condoms

used and caught in a wrinkle of leather and silk.
It snaps shut on a mirror, opens at the twist

of her fingers. Above all, it contains—archives,
embraces, protects. Envelops. There is no outside

to its outside, its round balls hold all the world,
and in its ducts the Milky Way. Finger each swirl

from the lidded eye: the *o* of how (as in power),
the *o* of come (as in money). No way out

beneath this burial dress, this baggage
mummifying daddy's little girl.

Promises / eye

It's the one I look
away

from.
One-eyed, his punch-

line catches in my
gut.

That
other centrifuge of

instinct coils and coils
inside:

punkish
pink and twisted. Soft

as knives, this lurched
gulp

taste
of sick of fistclench

bonecrack. Centre
screen

obscured
his tenderness: I've

seen him, head between
girl

thighs,
horsetongue lapping

clean water. His kind
knuckles

down
I guess. Back to work:

vitreous blade marks the
spot.

Can't
look. Want to. Come and see.

Nobody Knows / ankles

Slim ankles twitch
my evanescent cock.

The dream one, made of silver
and cone-shaped, held against

pubic bone by a chain slung
around my hips. Fragile,

as his filmic calves are,
the angle of his back

as it meets its own reflection.
Adolescent, his grave eyes

survey flesh in its newness and,
there, it jumps again. The phantom

thing, not phallic but some softer
word: slug, comforter, velvet scarf

nestled between numb thighs. For
months now, no feeling, clit withdrawn

into itself and frozen. Now what's swollen
is this: ghost-flesh, evanescence summoned

by absence. Shadows on a screen, mirror-
doubles. And my—I remember

the title as *Nobody's Home*. Abandon
meant. Empty skeleton whose bones

melt into the red plush seat, and sear
with spring. Awakening. No body

knows what sadness passed between
us and our reflections. In that silvered

gap, this softness forms: of afternoon,
of velvet, of downy limbs. And all desire's

gentleness caught here, this point crumbling
into its point like 4B lead. This ache

of having, chain strung eyes to ankles.
This thing hung glittering.

London Fashion Week / pelvis

stepping out
onto the sunset
catwalk, London

juts its bones in
couture: organza
sky distressed

over the West End's
knowing armour—it's
all about structure,

darling, the single
crane dangling its
ruby earring: blood

pendent amidst blue,
last drop on the map
wrapped and worn

as a dress; the full
moon is artless, a silver
given, a fluorescent

puffball scattering
glitter spores of desire
over the shards, ascendant

crystals healing only
sceptics: the hard city
softened by chiffons of

fog as it tries to rise,
a ten-inch heel spiking
the stars into the sky.

Zero / navel

The first day in rehearsal, not the first hour but sometime
towards late afternoon, when everything was edging almost
gold, we stopped

and held each others' cocks. Bare as it sounds, it was: pants
down warming overworked ankles, navels half-exposed against
ragged T-shirt hems

whose limning insistently caught the eye. Mirror work, body
    exchanged
for body against that gap of abdomen; cotton lifting from the core—
pivots the drop. Fulcrum

and then: nothing. Not erotic but. Work. Dancing, we must touch
each inch of the other. With confidence—and in as well. It's
a weighing-up,

a grip no different than lifting Sylvie at the waist, or a shovel. Spade's
a spade, and we have things—memories, their movements—to dig
out of one another

like fragments from a bombed city. We have to balance findings
against what's lost. It's limbic. Circulating. Pulsing, even; turned
out but not on, except

as lights are. Aware: body as story. On my knees: scars; his back
knobbed with brittle bone. And these, between us, excavation
and its tools,

evidence and wound. Breath catch and in. Evaluation. Paler, thinner,
veined, warmer, silken. Shy. All movement focused in on navel, on
notmoving. Holding

still.

PIEUVRES / LÈVRES (LILIES / LIPS)

Did I realise then that I would spend my whole life
with their lipstick on my face. Other girls and their kisses

goodbye. I know that now, having watched soft asses
walk away from me, having been paid my tithe

for watchful quiet. For the flattery of desire. Ingrown
hair, that's what it's like: turning against the razor

blade and on itself. Like my toes, curled mazily
through each other with waiting, waiting that flows

up my calves and out my mouth. A shower in reverse:
a fountain, inwards out. And what was in her,

I felt that too. All her hardness in my fingers
rattling her stem. All those flower words, perverse

euphemisms for a force like an ocean
in a swimming pool. Did she not see

what poured out of (her into) me? Salt of her sea,
stick of her sap. And it's not the explosion

that I'm talking about, her wet cunt a concrete
underpass around my hand. It's the light that thrums

from her lily-mouth, her pollinated tongue
extended like a stamen. Like a beesting hot-sweet

under the skin, a tear oozing from an eye. An ingrown
hair turning outwards against skin tough as petals

under drops of rain. The pain of it like cold metal,
like waiting. The stem of spit plunges down

and you wonder that such softness does such hurt.
No softness in the doing: spit's active as a limb,

a cock, a race, a city street. It dances itself thin.
The stem of things. Wet birth. My first.

www.ingramcontent.com/pod-product-compliance
Lightning Source LLC
Chambersburg PA
CBHW030047100426
42734CB00036B/576